Hot sunny days

Photography by John Pettitt

It is fun to play in water

on hot sunny days.

You can go to the pool
with your mom and dad.

They will look after you.
They will teach you to swim.

Rivers are dangerous.

Rivers are too dangerous
for boys and girls to swim in.

You can swim at some beaches.
Some waves are little,
and some waves are big.

Where is it safe to swim
at this beach?

On some days,

the sun can get very hot.

It is not good to play
in the hot sun.

You can put on a shirt.
You can put on a hat.

You can play in the shade.

You can play under trees.

It is fun to play
where it is safe.